Ezra Edwards Lamb

Sermon on the Death of President Lincoln

Preached in the Congregational Church of Rootstown

Ezra Edwards Lamb

Sermon on the Death of President Lincoln
Preached in the Congregational Church of Rootstown

ISBN/EAN: 9783337112943

Printed in Europe, USA, Canada, Australia, Japan

Cover: Foto ©Lupo / pixelio.de

More available books at **www.hansebooks.com**

SERMON

ON THE DEATH OF

President Lincoln

PREACHED IN THE CONGREGATIONAL CHURCH OF ROOTSTOWN,

By Rev. E. E. LAMB,

Sabbath Morning, April 23, 1865.

[PUBLISHED BY REQUEST.]

TEXT—1st Samuel, 1st Chapter, 25th Verse.—"How are the mighty fallen in the midst of battle! O Jonathan thou wast slain in thy high places."

THERE is mourning in the nation's capital. There is sorrow in the nation's heart. A mighty grief rests upon us. The crown has fallen from our heads. The true, the noble, and the great has gone. But yesterday the nation's heart was full of joy—to-day our speechless souls refuse their wonted consolation. But yesterday hope plumed her wings on all our mountains—to-day the murmur of sorrow wails through all our valleys. But yesterday peace with her attendant angels appeared in mid-heaven—but to-day clouds are wrapped around her feet. But yesterday men were divided in their opinion—to-day the iron of anguish has fused all hearts. But yesterday the nation's heart was magnanimous—to-day vengeance has come down from the Lord of hosts, and where men walked a few days ago with buoyant steps and hearts of mercy, *now* strong men walk with clenched fists and hearts of steel. One short whisper has revolutionized this whole land. God spoke, and we stood still. And why this change? Abraııam Lincoln is dead! The chosen of God was slain in his high places. Our Moses who has led us through these four wilderness years, has been summoned of God, and now the whole nation stands in tearful agony around the mount whither his feet have gone up. Our joy and our sorrow stand side by side in the great book of God. The cloud of incense all radiant with light, had a fringe of sackcloth. It was a dark morning that saw our President die. The heavens were weeping. The sun hid himself in shadows, and the angel who bore his great spirit aloft was muffled in clouds. Fit emblem of those mightier shadows which rested upon our hearts. Strong type of those holier tears which were shed by a loving and noble people.

The people's President and friend is dead, and it is proper in the calm light of this holy Sabbath that we call to mind the lessons of his life and death. Mr. Lincoln was most heartily a man of the people. Educated not in lordly halls, surrounded not with wealth and refinement. Taken from the circle of no hereditary greatness, he was cradled in the bosom of poverty. He was trained in the rough school of adversity. His hands were made to work—his mind was made to think. He had just that elementary training necessary to fit him to be a guide in our night of danger. In those master struggles with poverty, his mind was prepared to lead the destinies of a struggling nation. Adversity is the school of greatness. Great minds are rocked in the hammock of the storms. The leaders of grand developments need this strong preparation. It is the school of God. Contending in youth with obstacles, ribs the heart with oak. All successful leaders of revolutions have been thus educated. Moses, God's chosen, must go into the wilderness for many years, to get the necessary discipline to withstand the trials before him. Christ was born in the manger—he wandered on the mountains, that he might go in joy to his triumphant death. God prepares His own leaders. He commissions His own Captains. Angels of God stand around the cradle of those men whose feet are to bring good tidings.

Mr. Lincoln, whether splitting rails, or rowing a boat against the tide, or poring over some old grammar by the fireside, was preparing himself unconsciously for his great commission. His hands, hardened by toil, were being fitted to hold a world. The crown of God was shining from afar above his head. Was he splitting rails?—it was that his right arm might split in pieces the gigantic power of slavery. Was he rowing a flat-boat against the turgid waters of the Mississippi?—it was that he might row us successfully against the billows of this seething rebellion. His early toils were an earnest of his future greatness. Mr. Lincoln, coming from the people, had the instincts of the people. He knew us in every part. He was quick to understand the heart of the nation. And when our hearts beat, his beat with them. So quick were his sensibilities, that he seemed almost to hear our secret prayers for him. No sooner had our faintest wish become an earnest hope, before he seized upon it as a guiding principle. Hence he was a safe man. For the instincts of a Christian people are almost always right. God's providences bring an inspiration. And who shall catch that inspiration but Christian hearts? In times of great calamity the breathings of this inspiration in Christian souls are the voice of God. He that follows them, cannot go far astray. Mr. Lincoln followed them. He threw himself upon the Christian sentiment. "Pray for me," was his first proclamation to the American people. It was the key-note of his reign. He could not be otherwise than a safe man. For a man walks with firm step whose pathway is carpeted with prayer. Mr. Lincoln knew this. He knew that the twin angels of Faith and Hope staid up his hands. His great soul was exalted amid crushing responsibilities, for amid the darkest hours he slept on pillows of prayer. Such was his faith in the people, that he went no farther than their dictation. Hence he was a slow man. He believed in Democracy. He trusted in the heart of the Republic. He believed that there were righteous men enough to save us. He felt that God was greater than he—and that the spirit of freedom, born of our mountains, and nursed by our water-courses, was unconquerable. Standing in such reverence of the people, and with head uncovered before God, his career has seemed slow. We were impatient at his delay. But ah, his slowness was our salvation. God was gathering up His truth, and pouring it into his soul. God was a long time in whetting His sword of justice, before He put it in Abraham Lincoln's hand, but when He had put it there, it was keen as burnished lightning. Before the car of our salvation moved, the track was greased with tears. But when it did move, the track was torn up behind it. Standing on the mount of regeneration to-day—bathed in heaven's own light—we can now judge of events. God's arm is now uncovered, and we can see it holding the President back. He was slow to move, but when he did move, heaven with hallelujahs rang. When he did move, he took the ages with him. When he did move, *it was done.* He took no steps backwards, for there was no need of it. Great issues went forth from his mouth. But he would not retract. The millstone of war could not grind out a confession. Planted on the faith of the people, and the truth of God, he was immovable as the solid hills. Whatever may be said of Mr. Lincoln's abilities, he will be classed with the great statesmen of the world. Not because of his eloquence. Not because he has convulsed Senates by his magic powers. But because of his pure spiritual insight. He grasped with a firm conviction the issues of this war. He saw with a clear vision the truth involved. Not that he comprehended the greatness of the war at the beginning. What mortal man did? Four years ago, as the heavens muttered thunder, and the earth reeled with uncertain force—as this gigantic rebellion stood before us armed with terror—who measured its power? Who counted the tears that should fall to quench its thirst? Who numbered the heroes that should fall before it? Blame not Mr. Lincoln for not forecasting the magnitude of the war. God had it in His fists. None but a prophetic tongue of flame could have foretold it. The whole nation stood before the appalling reality *speechless.* The terrors of

Sinai were about us, and God came down clothed in darkness. At that hour when men stood trembling, and reason was dumb before the surging passions of the nation, our President saw with an angel's eye the truth. Although he measured not the greatness, yet he did comprehend the *cause* of the war.— Through all his acts he held fast to the righteousness of the struggle. He saw God, in the fight. So deep was the spirituality of his acts, that he secured the highest sympathy of good men. His voice was the voice of Jacob. His language was the language of Canaan. Hence he was the church's President. The church of every name gathered about him, as about the chosen of God. Good men loved him. Next to the name of the dear boy in the army, his name would be whispered in the silent closet. Heaven is full of prayer for him. If God had annointed him King in the presence of the universe, we could not have loved him more. On this account he was hated of bad men. All of the malignity precipitated by this war rose up against him. The filth and scum of our cities were ready to mob him. Assassins stood ready to murder him. He was the best loved and best hated man in the world. Mr. Lincoln did nothing to arouse such a storm of hate, only because he did right. So manly and true was he, that sin flamed before him. It was an honor for any man to be hated by such men. Let it be written on his tomb, "Here lies a man whom the devil hated." He needs no mightier eulogy. He needs no better immortality. Such was Mr. Lincoln's spiritual sagacity, that he was almost always right. In a period of most dire confusion, when there were no precedents to go by—when there was no certainty for the future—when the nation was groaning in death—when mighty armies were contending in the grip of death—when mighty and untried principles were to be established—at such an hour, when the heads of old statesmen were giddy with confusion, then it was that our simple minded President led forth like a stalwart warrior. He struck out into new and untried paths. He made bold strokes. He set forth new, yet majestic principles. He differed with his Cabinet. He differed with Congress.

He differed with the wisest men of the nation, and yet Abraham Lincoln was most always right. The sequel is, he was an honest man. He cared not for self. He followed one single honest purpose. The convictions of his heart were his revelations from God. His convictions of right were his star of Bethlehem that guided him where the Son of God lay. His eye was single, and his whole body was full of light. Hence Mr. Lincoln was a growing man. He was always open to conviction. He treasured up the lessons of the war. He believed that God had something to say in this contest, and he waited reverently to hear. And he did hear. No man in the nation grew faster than he. His first message was an appeal to the nation, his last was an appeal to God. No such words had ever been uttered by a President before, as the last message of Mr. Lincoln. They were penned beneath the throne of God. In the eyes of worldly wisdom his course may seem childish. It is considered folly for a great mind to change. But fools are unchangeable. Wisdom plumes her wings for a new flight every morning. It is the healthy tree that gets a fresh start every time that God's Spring passes over it. It is the dead tree that stands the same from year to year, and puts forth no leaves to catch sunbeams. It is true nobility to open the heart towards God. Mr. Lincoln opened his soul toward God. He was quick as a child to repent when wrong, but he was immutable, when right. He was ready to act upon new convictions. He had a heart that was profoundly impressed by the lessons of the war. Hence he was a type of our higher manhood—of a new order of men. This war has elevated the whole nation. And the President was a fit representative of our exaltation. Mr. Lincoln was by nature opposed to slavery. He had felt its debasing power. He had seen its withering blight. He had breathed the unchained air of our broad prairies. By his own right arm he had wrought out his own manhood. By the strength of a stalwart purpose he had written high his name, where God says, "This is a man." He rejoiced in his own liberty. He knew what there was in man. With such a training, and with such instincts, he was just the man to understand the contest with slavery. Had he been raised in affluence, liberty would have been to him only a theory. He would not have felt its glory. But now liberty was welded into his heart. It ran in his veins. Its music thrilled his soul. He was prepared to fight oppression. And well did he do it. He scented it in the smoke of battle. He hunted it, as if thirsting for its blood. To successfully combat error, some of its iron must have entered our souls. We must have known it. Men don't fight well for a bare theory. But O! the reality makes them terrible. The Lord of glory was not exempt from this great principle. That He might subdue all things unto Himself, He took hold of sin. He passed for a little time under its dominion, as the sun hides in clouds, only to come out radiant with victory. Christ tasted of death, that he might disenthrall man from its dominion. It took a Luther who had felt all the folly and blasphemy of Popery, to strike it to the heart. No other man could have thundered so loudly in the gates of hell. No other man could have sent it quivering to its death. It takes a Napoleon to govern France. He is called the man of destiny. Aristocrat Kings could not hold the reins of power. But Napoleon can. He was educated in prison. He lived with the common people. He knows what France needs; he has got hold of her heart. Hence he knows how to make destiny. It takes a Gough to lay open the horrors of intemperance. He has the key to the drunkard's dungeon. It was made out of his own blood. The darkness and the terror, the tremors and the demons are all known to him; hence his tongue flashes the reality. He dips his pen in his own soul. It takes a Brownlow to deal with slavery. He knows it. Its mold and its curse rest upon him. Its eternal blight broods through all his being. Let him curse it, let him slay it; he is only bringing forth fruits meet for repentance. Those are the most terrible avengers which a wicked cause itself produces. But it took Abraham Lincoln to subdue slavery. Springing from the noble yeomanry of our land, hearing the birds singing their sweet songs of liberty, he was God's chosen avenger. His free and noble spirit was not the spirit of our cities. Cities are most always oppressive. The air of ignorance and corruption mingle in the atmosphere of cities. Mr. Lincoln had no foreign element in his heart. He caught his inspiration from our institutions. His spirit was the spirit of our mountains, the spirit of our prairies, the spirit of our lakes and rivers, the spirit of our storms! Free, grandly free and glorious. He was a genuine American. The same spirit of freedom is born of the plow and the hammer. The anvil, the hammer, and the axe ring the death knell of tyranny. Nothing a tyrant so much fears as the calloused hand of a freeman. It was not then so much the President that signed the death-warrant of slavery as the spirit of freemen acting through him. He blew the trumpet with the nation's breath. The very air we breathed demanded its destruction, and God said "amen." Mr. Lincoln was one of the people. His great, good heart the people felt. Mutual sympathy made us mutual friends. In the darkest hour the people turned to him with the firmest confidence. They looked to "Father Abraham" with implicit trust. His name like a skillful hand evoked harmony from all the nobler chords of our being. He had called for great sacrifices from us. He had demanded our heart's treasures. By his order the jewel has been plucked from many households. But he only took our jewels that he might perfect the diadem of the nation. He picked our roses that he might present to God our country's glorious wreath of immortelles. Those who sacrificed the most, loved him the most. The brave old soldier shouted above his camp fire, "God bless Abraham Lincoln." The wounded hero, writhing in his pains, prayed, "God bless Abraham Lincoln," and the lone widow, checking her tears, took up the same prayer. His homely name became a magic word. It called forth cheers wherever spoken. It became an emblem of our nation's glory. He had carried away the largest half of the nation's heart. Such affection does sorrow forge. We cannot forget those who walk with us in the vale of shadows. Angels bind our hearts with gold when we suffer together. In this long night of our woe he went with us. In this furnace

..LINCOLN..

COMPILED BY

EDWARD S. JOHNSON
CUSTODIAN

..1903..

ABRAHAM LINCOLN

AND HIS

LAST RESTING PLACE.

A LEAFLET PUBLISHED FOR DISTRIBUTION

...AT THE...

NATIONAL LINCOLN MONUMENT

SPRINGFIELD, ILLINOIS.

The Life of Abraham Lincoln has been written by many men in many tongues.

The resources of rhetoric and eloquence have been exhausted in their portrayal of this character that however viewed holds a lesson for all mankind.

In this brief space and for the purpose which this leaflet is designed to serve, the simple homely details of the martyred President's early life could not be better told than in his own words. No polished recital could be so prized by the great multitude who hold his memory dear as this transcript of a letter written in 1859 to his friend the Hon. Jesse W. Fell of Bloomington, Illinois :

I was born Feb. 12. 1809, in Hardin County, Kentucky. My parents were both born in Virginia, of undistinguished families — second families perhaps I should say. My mother, who died in my tenth year, was of a family of the name of Hanks, some of whom now reside in Adams, and others in Macon counties, Illinois — My paternal grandfather, Abraham Lincoln, emigrated from Rockingham County, Virginia, to Kentucky, about 1781 or 2, where, a year or two later, he was killed by indians, not in battle, but by stealth, when he was laboring to open a farm in the forest — His ancestors, who were quakers, went to Virginia from Berks county, Pennsylvania — An effort to identify them with the New-England family of the same name ended in nothing more definite, than a similarity of christian names in both families, such as Enoch, Levi, Mordecai, Solomon, Abraham, and the like —

My father, at the death of his father, was but six years of age; and he grew up, litterally without education. He removed from Kentucky to what is now Spencer county, Indiana, in my eighth year — We reached our new home about the time the State came into the Union — It was a wild region, with many bears and other wild animals, still in the woods — There I grew up — There were some schools, so called; but no qualification was ever required of a teacher, beyond "readin, writin, and cipherin" to the Rule of Three — If a straggler supposed to understand latin, happened to sojourn in

the neighborhood, he was looked upon as a
wizzard— There was absolutely nothing to excite
ambition for education. Of course when I came of
age I did not know much— Still somehow, I could
read, write, and cipher to the Rule of Three, but
that was all— I have not been to school since—
The little advance I now have upon this store of education, I have had picked up from time to time under
the pressure of necessity—

I was raised to farm work, which I continued
till I was twentytwo— At twentyone I came to
Illinois, and passed the first year in Illinois—
Macon County— Then I got to New Salem (at that time
in Sangamon, now in Menard County, where I remained a year as a sort of Clerk in a
store— Then came the Black Hawk war;
and I was elected a Captain of Volunteers—
a success which gave me more pleasure
than any I have had since— I went the
campaign, was elated, ran for the Legislature the
same year (1832) and was beaten— the only time
I ever have been beaten by the people— The next,
and three succeeding biennial elections, I was elected to the Legislature— I was not a candidate
afterwards. During this Legislative period I had
studied law, and removed to Springfield to
make practice it— In 1846 I was once elected
to the lower House of Congress— Was not a candidate for re-election— From 1849 to 1854, both

inclusive, practiced law more assiduously than ever before — Always a whig in politics, and generally on the whig electoral tickets, making active canvasses — I was losing interest in politics, when the repeal of the Missouri Compromise aroused me again. What I have done since then is pretty well known.

If any personal description of me is thought desirable, it may be said, I am, in height, six feet, four inches, nearly; lean in flesh, weighing, on an average, one hundred and eighty pounds; dark complexion, with coarse black hair, and grey eyes — no other marks or brands recollected —

Hon. J. W. Fell.

Yours very truly
A. Lincoln

Washington. D.C. March 20. 18½

We the undersigned hereby certify that the foregoing statement is in the hand writing of Abraham Lincoln.

David Davis
Lyman Trumbull
Charles Sumner

Abraham Lincoln little thought as he penned the words, "What I have done since then is pretty well known," that a world would one day listen enthralled to the tale of what he had done and should do in the decade from 1855 to 1865.

In 1854 the repeal of the Missouri Compromise of 1820 opened a new political era, and an agitation of the slavery question was begun which was destined to grow until the shackles were struck forever from the hands of the slave.

By this repeal slavery claimed protection everywhere; it sought to nationalize itself. At this time the question of "popular sovereignty" arose, the right of the people of a territory to choose their own institutions, and upon this question Mr. Lincoln and Mr. Douglas fought the "battle of the giants," and Mr. Lincoln's signal ability as an orator was forever established. He became at once the leader of his party in the West and the foremost champion of the liberties of the oppressed.

In a private letter, written at this time, Mr. Lincoln defines his position on the great question of the day as follows:

"I acknowledge your rights and my obligations under the constitution in regard to your slaves. I confess I hate to see the poor creatures hunted down and caught and carried back to their stripes and unrequited toil, but I keep quiet. You ought to appreciate how much the great body of the people of the North crucify their feelings in order to maintain their loyalty to the Constitution and the Union. I *do* oppose the *extension* of slavery because my judgment and feelings so prompt me, and I am under no obligations to the contrary. As a nation we began by declaring 'all men are created equal.' We now practically read it, 'all men are created equal except negroes.' When it comes to making wholesale exceptions I should prefer emigrating to some country where they make no pretense of loving liberty, where despotism can be taken pure without the base alloy of hypocrisy.
Your friend,

A. LINCOLN."

May 29, 1856, the Republican party of Illinois was organized, and he was now the leader of a party whose avowed purpose it was to resist the extension of slavery. At the national convention his name was presented as a candidate for vice-president. He did not receive the required number of votes, but the action was complimentary and served as Mr. Lincoln's formal introduction to the nation.

The senatorial campaign of 1858 in Illinois was memorable for the questions involved and for the debates between Douglas and Lincoln upon the great issues that were even then distracting the nation. When these two met in intellectual combat the nation paused to listen. "The eyes of all the eastern states were turned to the west where young republicanism and old democracy were establishing the dividing lines and preparing for the great struggle soon to begin.

To say that Mr. Lincoln was the victor in the contest morally and intellectually is simply to record the judgment of the world.

COPYRIGHT 1901 BY GUY R MATHIS

TEMPORARY TOMB.

His speeches were clear, logical, powerful and exhaustive. On these his reputation as an orator and debator rest. They defined the difference between the power of slavery and the policy of freedom which ended, after expenditures of uncounted treasure and unmeasured blood, in the final overthrow of the institution of slavery.

Mr. Lincoln was defeated in this campaign and Mr. Douglas was returned to the Senate, but Mr. Lincoln was now thoroughly committed to politics. In 1859 and 1860 he journeyed in the Eastern states, making speeches that thrilled and electrified the audiences which he had expected to find cold and critical.

The mutterings of secession already filled the land. The spirit of unrest and rebellion was gaining ground, but wherever the voice of Lincoln was heard it was pleading for union, for peace, for the Constitution, deprecating the evils of slavery as it existed and protesting against its extension into free states and territories.

His was the voice of one crying in the wilderness, warning the men of the North and the South that a house divided against itself cannot stand. On the 16th of June, 1860, Mr. Lincoln received the nomination of the republican convention held at Chicago for President of the United States. How this plain, comparatively unknown Illinois lawyer was chosen in this critical hour before a man like Seward, with his wide experience and acquaintance, his large influence and surpassing ability, his name and fame of thirty years standing, must be regarded as the guiding of that Providence that had brooded over the life of the republic since it declared itself to be the home of the free, the refuge of the oppressed. On the 6th of November Mr. Lincoln was elected, by a handsome plurality, President of the United States.

At eight o'clock Monday morning, February 11, 1861, Mr. Lincoln left Springfield for the National Capital to enter upon his duties as President. With these simple words he took leave of his friends and neighbors:

"My friends: No one not in my position can appreciate the sadness I feel at this parting. To this people I owe all that I am. Here I have lived more than a quarter of a century; here my children were born, and here one of them lies buried. I know not how soon I shall see you again. A duty devolves upon me which is perhaps greater than that which has devolved upon any other man since the days of Washington. He never would have succeeded except by the aid of Divine Providence, upon which he at all times relied. I feel that I cannot succeed without the same Divine aid which sustained him, and on the same Almighty Being I place my reliance for support, and I hope you, my friends, will all pray that I may receive that Divine assistance without which I cannot succeed but with which success is certain. Again I bid you an affectionate farewell."

These proved to be his last words to Springfield auditors.

The result of this election pleased and united the North while it angered the South. To the more thoughtful men of both parties a crisis seemed imminent. The southern states immediately seceded; the Southern Confederacy was formed with Jefferson Davis as President;

forts and arsenals were seized and the war of the rebellion fairly inaugurated. It was this disrupted Union, this all but shattered government, which waited for the man who upon the 4th day of March, 1861, took the oath of office and became the President of the United States.

The closing words of his memorable inaugural address must have convinced his listeners of the wisdom, the strength, the gentleness of this new incumbent of the chair of State:

"In your hands, my dissatisfied fellow countrymen, and not in mine, is the momentous issue of civil war. The government will not assail you. You can have no conflict without being yourselves the aggressors. You have no oath registered in Heaven to destroy the government, while I shall have the most solemn one to preserve, protect and defend it. I am loth to close. We are not enemies, but friends. The mystic cords of memory, stretching from every battlefield and patriot grave to every living heart and hearthstone all over this broad land will yet swell the chorus of the Union when again touched, as they surely will be, by the better angels of our nature."

With infinite patience and unequaled forbearance and sagacity, Mr. Lincoln strove to avert war, but when, on April 12, 1861, the rebel batteries were opened upon Fort Sumpter, forbearance was no longer possible, and, on the 15th day of April, the pen that had only been used to counsel moderation, to urge loyalty, penned a proclamation calling for seventy-five thousand men and the Civil War was begun. The popular government had been called an experiment. Two points of the experiment had already been settled: The government had been established and it had been administered. One point remained to be established: Its successful maintenance against a formidable internal attempt to overthrow it. Congress ably supported Mr. Lincoln. It placed at his disposal five million dollars and gave him liberty to call out half a million men. During all the years of that long, sad war there were loyal hearts among his admirers that held up the hands of their President, but the crowning personality, the strong, pervading, directing, controlling spirit was that of Abraham Lincoln, whether watching the progress of events from his almost beleagured capital or while visiting and mingling with his army at the front.

Never for a moment did he lay aside his personal responsibility. Never did he swerve from his resolve, expressed in the words of his memorable speech at the dedication of the soldiers' graves at Gettysburg:

"We have come to dedicate a portion of this field as a final resting place for those who here gave their lives that the nation might live. But, in a larger sense, we cannot dedicate, we cannot consecrate, we cannot hallow this ground. The brave men living and dead who struggled here have consecrated it far beyond our power to add or detract. The world will little note nor long remember what we say here, but it can never forget what they did here. It is for us, the living, rather to be dedicated here to the unfinished work which they who fought here have so nobly advanced. It is rather for us to be here dedicated to the great task remaining before us, that from these honored dead we take increased devotion to that cause for which they gave the last full measure of devotion, that we here highly resolve that these

INFANTRY GROUP.

CAVALRY GROUP.

ARTILLERY GROUP.

NAVAL GROUP.

dead shall not have died in vain; that this nation, under God, shall have a new birth of freedom and that government of the people, by the people and for the people shall not perish from the earth."

The story of the war and the life of Lincoln are inseparable. The recital of all those years of marching, camping, fighting, of wounds, privations, victory, defeat and death cannot be made without the story of Lincoln interwoven into its warp and woof. The days fraught with the grave issues of the war went by, victory alternating with defeat until, in the judgment of the commander-in-chief, the time had come to emancipate the colored race.

Early in August of 1863, President Lincoln called a meeting of his Cabinet and submitted for their consideration the original draft of his Emancipation Proclamation. On the 1st day of January, 1864, Mr. Lincoln issued the final Proclamation of Emancipation, bringing freedom to four million of slaves and removing forever from the land he loved the blot of slavery.

It seemed fitting that to this man who had blazed the way through the wilderness for this cause, who had brooded and smarted under the sense of the sin of slavery from his early untaught youth, who in clarion tones had declared, at the outset of his career, that he "would speak for freedom against slavery until everywhere in all this broad land the sun shall shine, the rain shall fall and the wind shall blow upon no man who goes forth to unrequited toil." It was meet that from his lips should fall the words that made four million men free, and it is in consonance with the character of the great Emancipator that in this supreme moment of his life he reverently invoked upon that act "the considerate judgment of mankind and the gracious favor of Almighty God."

The latter part of the year 1863 was marked by the success of Union armies. The Republican National Convention assembled in Baltimore, June 8, 1864, unanimously nominated Mr. Lincoln as their candidate for President. His words accepting this nomination were characteristic:

"Having served four years in the depths of a great and yet unended national peril, I can view this call to a second term in no wise more flattering to myself than as an expression of the public judgment that I may better finish a difficult work than could any one less severely schooled to the task. In this view, and with assured reliance on that Almighty Ruler who has so graciously sustained us thus far, and with increased gratitude to the generous people for their continued confidence, I accept the renewed trust with its yet onerous and perplexing duties and responsibilities."

During the height of the canvass President Lincoln issued a call for five hundred thousand men, also making provisions for a draft if necessary. His friends feared that this measure might cost him his election, but he waived that aside as he always did personal consideration that might conflict with duty.

November came, and with it Mr. Lincoln's re-election. His second election proved the death blow to the rebellion. From that time the Southern armies never gained a substantial victory. When the

12

Thirty-Eighth Congress assembled December 6, 1864, President Lincoln recommended an amendment to the Constitution making human slavery forever impossible in the United States.

The joint resolutions for the extinction of slavery passed Congress and received the signature of the President January 31, 1865. The legislature of Illinois, being then in session, took up the question at once and in less than twenty-four hours after its passage by Congress Mr. Lincoln had the satisfaction of receiving a telegram from his old home announcing the fact that the constitutional amendment had been ratified by both houses of the legislature of his own state February 1, 1865. The action of the legislatures of other states soon followed, and thus was completed and confirmed the work of the proclamation of emancipation.

Upon the 4th of March, 1865, Mr. Lincoln was for the second time inaugurated.President of the United States. His inaugural address upon that occasion has become a classic. Its closing words have been quoted wherever the foot of an American has strayed beneath the sun. "Fondly do we hope, reverently do we pray that this mighty scourge of war may speedily pass away, yet, if God wills that it continue until all the wealth piled by the bondsman's two hundred and fifty years of unrequited toil shall be sunk, and until every drop of blood drawn by the lash shall be paid by another drawn by the sword, as was said three thousand years ago, so still it must be said, the judgments of the Lord are true and righteous altogether. With malice toward none, with charity for all, with firmness in the right as God gives us to see the right, let us strive to finish the work we are in, to bind up the nation's wounds, to care for him who shall have borne the battle, to do all which may achieve and cherish a just and lasting peace among ourselves and with all nations."

The closing scenes of the war were being enacted in quick succession. Richmond had fallen, and on the 4th day of April, just one month after his second inauguration, President Lincoln, leading his little son by the hand, entered the vanquished city on foot. Never has the world seen a more modest conqueror, a more characteristic triumphal procession. No army with banners and drums, only a few of those who had been slaves escorting the victorious chief with benedictions and tears into the capital of the fallen foe.

A few more days brought the surrender of Lee's army and peace was assured. Everywhere festive guns were booming, bells pealing, churches ringing with thanksgivings.

The 14th of April was the anniversary of the fall of Sumpter. President Lincoln had ordered that day to be signalized by restoring the old flag to its place on the shattered ramparts of Fort Sumpter. He ordered the same faithful hands that pulled it down to raise it— every battery that fired upon it should salute it. Said the Rev. Henry Ward Beecher upon that occasion: "From this pulpit of broken stone we send to the President of the United States our solemn congratulations that God has sustained his life and health under the unparalleled hardships and suffering of four bloody years and permitted him to behold this auspicious consummation of that national unity for which he has labored with such disinterested wisdom."

13

But, before the kindly words had flashed over the telegraph wires to the ears of the patient man in whose honor they were spoken, the bullet of the assassin had done its work. The sad words, "I feel a presentiment that I shall not outlast the rebellion; when it is over my work will be done," were verified, and all civilized mankind stood mourning around the bier of the dead President. Then began that unparalleled funeral procession, a mournful pageant, passing country and village and city, winding along the territories of vast states along a track of fifteen hundred miles, carrying the revered dead back to his own people, to the scenes of his early life, back to the prairies of Illinois. Said Beecher in his eloquent and touching funeral oration:

"Four years ago, oh, Illinois, we took from your midst an untried man from among the people. Behold! we return to you a mighty conqueror, not ours any more, but the nation's. Not ours but the world's. Give him place, oh ye prairies. In the midst of this great continent his dust shall rest, a sacred treasure to the myriads who shall come as pilgrims to that shrine to kindle anew their zeal and patriotism. Humble child of the backwoods, boatman, hired laborer, clerk, surveyor, captain, legislator, lawyer, debator, politician, orator, statesman, president, saviour of the republic, true Christian, true man. We receive thy life and its immeasurably great results as the choicest gifts that have ever been bestowed upon us; grateful to thee for thy truth to thyself, to us and to God; and grateful to that ministry of Providence which endowed thee so richly and bestowed thee upon the nation and mankind."

THE MONUMENT.

The body of Abraham Lincoln was deposited in the receiving vault at Oak Ridge cemetery May 4, 1865.

Upon the 11th of May, 1865, the National Lincoln Monument Association was formed, its object being to construct a monument to the memory of Abraham Lincoln in the city of Springfield, Ill.

The names of the gentlemen comprising the Lincoln Monument Association in 1865 were as follows:

Gov. Richard Oglesby,	Sharon Tyndale,
Orlin H. Miner,	Thomas J. Dennis,
John T. Stuart,	Newton Bateman,
Jesse K. DuBois,	S. H. Treat,
James C. Conkling,	O. M. Hatch,
John Williams,	S. H. Melvin,
Jacob Bunn,	James H. Beveridge,

David L. Phillips.

The temporary vault was built and the body of President Lincoln removed from the receiving vault of the cemetery on December 21, 1865. The body was placed in the crypt of the monument September 19, 1871, and was placed in the sarcophagus in the center of the catacomb October 9, 1874.

Owing to the instability of the earth under its foundations and its unequal settling the structure had begun to show signs of disintegration, neccessitating taking it down and rebuilding it from the foundation. The work was begun by Col. J. S. Culver in Nov., 1899, and finished June 1, 1901. A cemented vault was made beneath the floor of the catacomb directly underneath the sarcophagus and in this vault the body of President Lincoln was placed Sept. 26, 1901, where it will probably remain undisturbed forever.

The monument is built of brick and Quincy granite, the latter material only appearing in view. It consists of a square base 72½ feet on each side and 15 feet, 10 inches high. At the north side of the base is a semi-circular projection, the interior of which has a radius of 12 feet. It is the vestibule of the catacomb, and gives access to view the crypts in which are placed the bodies of Mr. Lincoln's wife and sons and his grandson, Abraham Lincoln, son of Hon. Robert T. Lincoln. On the south side of the base is another semi-circular projection of the same size, but this is continued .into the base so as to produce a room of elliptical shape, which is called Memorial Hall. Thus the base measures, including these two projections, 119½ feet from north to south and 72½ feet from east to west. In the angles formed by the addition of these two projections are handsome flights of stone steps, two on each end. These steps are protected by granite balustrades, which extend completely around the top of the base, which forms a terrace. From the plane of this terrace rises the obelisk, or die, which is 28 feet, 4 inches high from the ground, and tapered to 11 feet square at the top. At the angles of this die are four pedestals of 11 feet diameter, rising 12½ feet above the plane of the terrace. This obelisk, including the area occupied by the pedestals, is 41 feet square, while from the obelisk rises the shaft, tapering to 8 feet square at the summit. Upon the four pedestals stand the four bronze groups, representing the four arms of the service—infantry, cavalry, artillery and navy. Passing around the whole obelisk and pedestal is a band or chain of shields, each representing a state, the name of which is carved upon it. At the south side of the obelisk is a square pedestal, 7 feet high, supporting the statue of Lincoln, the pedestal being ornamented with the coat of arms of the United States. This coat of arms, in the position it occupies on the monument, is intended to typify the constitution of the United States. Mr. Lincoln's statue on the pedestal above it marks the whole an illustration of his position at the outbreak of the rebellion. He took his stand on the constitution as his authority for using the four arms of the war power of the government, the infantry, cavalry, artillery and navy, to hold together the states which are represented still lower on the monument by a cordon of tablets linking them together in a perpetual bond of union.

The money used in the original construction of this handsome monument came from the people by voluntary contributions. The first entry made by the treasurer of the association was May 8, 1865, and was from Isaac Reed, of New York, $100. Then came contributions from sunday schools, lodges, army associations, individuals and states. The Seventy-Third Regiment, United States colored troops, at New Orleans, contributed $1,437, a greater amount than was given by any other individual or organization except the State of Illinois. Many pages of the record are filled with the contributions from the Sunday schools of the land, and of the 5,145 entries, 1,697 are from Sunday schools. The largest part of the money was contributed in 1865, but it continued to come to the treasurer from all parts of the country until

1871. About $8,000 was contributed by the colored soldiers of the United States army. Only three states made appropriations for this fund—Illinois, $50,000; Missouri, $1,000 and Nevada $500.

The monument was dedicated October 15, 1874, the occasion being signalized by a tremendous outpouring of the people, the oration commemorative of the life and public services of the great emancipator being delivered by Governor Richard J. Oglesby. President Grant also spoke briefly on that occasion, and a poem was read by James Judson Lord.

The monument was built after the accepted designs of Larkin G. Mead, of Florence, Italy, and stands upon an eminence in Oak Ridge cemetery, occupying about nine acres of ground. Ground was broken on the site September 10, 1869, in the presence of 3,000 persons. The capstone was placed in position on May 22, 1871.

In July, 1871, citizens of Chicago, through Hon. J. Young Scammon, contributed $13,700 to pay for the Infantry group of statuary. In the city of New York, under the leadership of Gov. E. D. Morgan, 137 gentlemen subscribed and paid $100 each, amounting to $13,700, for the Naval group.

Of the four groups of statuary, the Naval Group was the first completed. This group represents a scene on the deck of a gunboat. The mortar is poised ready for action; the gunner has rolled up a shell ready for firing; the boy, or powder monkey, climbs to the highest point and is peering into the distance; the officer in command is about to examine the situation through his telescope.

The Infantry group was the next to reach Springfield. Both these groups were placed in position on the monument in September, 1877. The Infantry group represents an officer, a private soldier and a drummer, with arms and accoutrements, marching in expectation of battle. The officer in command raises the flag with one hand and, pointing to the enemy with the other, orders a charge. The private with the musket, as the representative of the whole line, is in the act of executing the charge. The drummer boy has become excited, lost his cap, thrown away his haversack and drawn a revolver to take part in the conflict.

The Artillery group represents a piece of artillery in battle. The enemy has succeeded in directing a shot so well as to dismount the gun. The officer in command mounts his disabled piece and with drawn saber fronts the enemy. The youthful soldier, with uplifted hands, is horrified at the havoc around him. The wounded and prostrate soldier wears a look of intense agony.

The Cavalry group, consisting of two human figures and a horse, represents a battle scene. The horse, from whose back the rider has just been thrown, is frantically rearing. The wounded and dying trumpeter, supported by a comrade, is bravely facing death. Each of these groups cost $13,700.

The statue of Mr. Lincoln stands on a pedestal projecting from the south side of the obelisk. This is the central figure in the group, or series of groups. As we gaze upon this heroic figure the mute lips seem again to speak in the memorable words that are now immortal. We hear again the ringing sentences spoken in 1859 of the slave power: "Broken by it, I too, may be; bow to it, I never will. * * If ever I feel the soul within me elevate and expand to those dimensions not wholly unworthy of its almighty architect, it is when I contemplate the cause of my country deserted by all the world beside, and I, standing up boldly and alone, hurling defiance at her victorious oppressors. Here, without contemplating consequences, before high Heaven and in the face of the world, I swear eternal fidelity to the just cause, as I deem it, of the land of my life, my liberty and my love.''

From the day of its dedication, October 15, 1874, until July 9, 1895, the Lincoln Monument remained in the control of the National Monument Association.

In 1874, after its dedication, John Carroll Power was made custodian, and continued in that position until his death in January, 1894. A sketch of the Lincoln Monument could not, in fairness, be written without paying a tribute to his faithfulness, zeal and love. He revered the nation's hero and gave to his last resting place the tenderest and most assiduous care. Much that is of interest in the history of this first decade of the existence of the monument has been written by his untiring pen that would otherwise have been lost.

After the attempt was made to steal the body of President Lincoln, Mr. Power summoned to his aid, in 1880, eight gentlemen, residents of Springfield, who organized as the "Lincoln Guard of Honor." They were J. Carroll Power, deceased; Jasper N. Reece, deceased; Gustavus S. Dana; James F. McNeill; Joseph P. Lindley; Edward S. Johnson; Horace Chapin; Noble B. Wiggins, deceased, and Clinton L. Conkling. Their object was to guard the precious dust of Abraham Lincoln from vandal hands and to conduct, upon the anniversaries of his birth and death, suitable memorial exercises.

During these years an admittance fee of twenty-five cents was required of all visitors to the monument, and this small fee constituted a fund by which the custodian was paid and the necessary expenses of the care of the grounds defrayed.

In the winter of 1894, in response to a demand voiced almost universally by the press and the people of Illinois, the general assembly made provision for the transfer of the National Lincoln Monument and grounds to the permanent care and custody of the state. The new law puts the monument into the charge of a board of control, consisting of the Governor of the State, the State Superintendent of Public Instruction and the State Treasurer.

July 9, 1895, Hon. Richard J. Oglesby, the President, the only surviving member of the original Lincoln Monument Association, turned over to the state, as represented by its chief executive, Governor Altgeld, the deeds and papers relating to the monument and grounds. The governor received the trust on behalf of the state, pledging its faithfulness to the duty of guarding and caring for the last resting place of the illustrious dead. The commission appointed as custodian Edward S. Johnson, major of the veteran 7th Illinois Infantry and a member of the Lincoln Guard of Honor. The admittance fee is a thing of the past and "To this Mecca of the people let all the people come, bringing garlands of flowers, carrying away lessons of life. There is no shrine more worthy of a devotee, no academy of the porch or grove where is taught so simply and so grandly the principles of greatness. Strew flowers, but bear away the imprint of his life, the flower of manliness and the wreath of honor."†

In the two score years since the death of Abraham Lincoln the scars of war have healed, the peace and unity for which he prayed have been realized, and it seems fitting to bring this brief recital of his life and the story of the strife from which it is inseparable up to date with this glance at the present:

"I have seen the new South! But I saw it not by the Potomac, nor by the Cumberland. I saw it by the shores of that peaceful lake whose waters are broad enough to carry the fleets of the world and deep enough to bury in its bosom all the hatred and all the sorrows of the past. I saw the new South, with her helmet on, bowing to the august Present.

"She had not forgotten the Past, but was bravely giving herself to a welcoming Future. There is a great city in the North, known all over as the type of restless, eager, business activity. Behold, on one day every shop and store and factory was closed! The hum of trade was hushed! The pulse of traffic had ceased to beat! And all this was because Chicago, gathering her own dead to her heart, found room for the brothers who wore the gray. Longstreet and Lee and Hampton sat at her hearths while the bugle and the drum proclaimed the everlasting peace.

"When the monument which marks the tomb of the Confederate dead at Oakwoods was dedicated, North and South marched together in streets thronged not with enemies but friends.

"Remembering their own heroic dead, the North reverently uncovered while the South gave tears and flowers to her's.

"The new South stood in line with the new North, and above them both towered a form brave, puissant, serene and free. IT WAS THE NEW NATION."*

---

*From George R. Peck's oration before the University of Virginia, June, 1895.

†Rev. Roswell O. Post's oration at the tomb of Lincoln, April, 1883.

The compiler wishes to acknowledge indebtedness to J. G. Holland's Life of Lincoln.

blast of God his form was seen. No other name will thrill us like his. It is locked up with our tears in God. And time cannot rust these things which God takes. The day is breaking. The herald comes with his beautiful feet upon the mountains, declaring that the night is past. Abraham Lincoln's fame is secure. It is carved deep in the corner-stone of a regenerated country. These thoughts explain the greatness of our sorrow. The whole nation stood still when the President died. Love smote us speechless. We were all mourners. Words, we had none. We could only look up into the darkened skies in astonishment. Our hearts refused to be comforted. This war has sent countless shafts of anguish through the land, but none like this. A dark shadow flitted over our households. A nameless agony sat down on our hearthstones. All business was suspended. Little children ran crying in the streets. Strong men bowed in uncontrollable grief. Columbia was in tears. There was wailing in all the borders thereof. The bells of God's temples sent up their clanging wail, and the priests of the Most High stood in tears by the altar. Sublimer than a nation in arms, was a nation in tears. What grander chariot could carry a hero to heaven than the mighty wings of a nation's anguish. He bore the weight of our sorrows when living; he has borne up to God the weight of our love. And what can be the sorrows of the freed slaves? What bitter tears will they shed upon the tomb of the great Emancipator. How green will they keep the grass over his head. In their rude calendar the name of Abraham Lincoln stands next to that of God. God sent the war, and Lincoln broke the chains. No sorrow is like their sorrow. His prairie grave will be the Mecca of their hopes, whither millions of dusky freemen will go to catch fresh inspiration. In their hearts his name will bloom in immortal vigor. Every dust over his head will be precious as pure gold. Oh! what a glorious immortality! In thinking of his life, we can truly say that he was a great man. Not great in learning and ability. But great in moral sentiment. Great in heart. Great in his unconsciousness. Even his familiar jokes were pointed with

diamonds. In all his public duties and tremendous responsibilities, he never got above the common people. With vice
all about him, he never lost his great manly heart. And his
eye never beamed with a sublimer goodness, and his heart
never heaved with a nobler impulse, than on the very day he
was murdered. That day his joyful eye looked over the South,
and he longed to take them to the nation's bosom. And when
he was murdered they took the angel of mercy from between
the cherubims. And what of his death? He died not for
himself. He was the embodiment of our new-born freedom.
A new idea was born of this war. An idea of freedom and
glory. Mr. Lincoln was its head and exponent. It was not
his life that was struck at. No one could have had vengeance
against him. They struck at the idea through him. They
wanted to strangle the life of new-born America. It was hatred against the child Jesus. It was the singing of the angels
and the promise of the dawn that created a thirst for blood.
That pistol ball that smote the President was a shot at truth.
That gleaming dagger was meant for every man, woman and
child in the land that loves the right. Poor fools, to think
that they could stop the rush of giant forces. That they could
pluck up the seeds which God has planted. That they could
blunt the sword of justice when God had polished it with
blood. That they could obstruct the way of the nation, as she
marched with a proud heart and firm step after the martial
drum beat of her destiny. O! what despicable folly! The
President dies, but the Republic lives. They might have destroyed an empire, where one man is the nation. But a nation where every man is President, cannot be destroyed. The
crowns that God gives, no man can take away. God has
crowned this nation with a new life—with a new glory. The
heart of truth does not depend on flesh and blood. It is immortal as Jehovah. If this war could not kill us, the gates of
hell cannot prevail against us. Supposing that they could
murder every freeman in the land. Our American idea would
not die. Supposing they should pick the bones of every hero

from our soil, and cast them into the sea. Truth would live.
Could they scrape up every particle of our land, and strain
every drop of patriot blood out of it, and throw it to the winds,
Liberty still lives! The very air has carried the inspiration
of this war around the globe. The souls of martyrs have
borne it up to God. You must dethrone Jehovah, before you
can behead liberty. What abject nonsense to strike at a gigantic idea with a pistol ball. How many think that the truth
will suffer by the death of Mr. Lincoln? It may suffer, but it
cannot be laid in the tomb with him. While we had confidence in his ability, and should have rejoiced to have had him
lived till the grand consummation, yet his life was not essen-
tial to the truth. Any cause is superlatively weak that de-
pends upon the life of one man. It was the time and manner
of his death that so mightily depressed the nation. We had
just shouted "hosannah." Victory was won. We heard the
angels singing peace. But before the magic strains of our
joy had reached heaven, a minor was heard. The chieftain
fell, where the drums were beating. Three days before Jesus
was slain, he rode into Jerusalem amid shouting hosannas,
and palm branches thrown in the way. But O! what a shock
to his disciples was his tragical death, following so soon! All
their hopes were carried to the grave with him. But truth
never was so strong as when Jesus was sleeping in the tomb.
It was a giant at sleep. America was never so mighty as
when Abraham Lincoln breathed his last. As he slowly
breathed out his last, God breathed o'er all our mountains.
As his life's blood flowed down, an invisible power flowed into
our hearts. It was a power born of calamity. It was the
consecration of sacrifice. Fear not, then, O Patriot! Old
battle clouded Columbia is safe. God, whom the winds obey,
holds us in his palms. The new soul which our father-land
has, shall persevere. Our struggling faith shall triumph
Poor, impotent, revengeful savages may starve our heroes, and
assassinate our chieftains, but the car of our hopes is headed
forward, and onward is the watchword of heaven. The wrath
of men shall become only praise.

12

Mr. Lincoln fell a victim to slavery. His death was the last stroke of the expiring rebellion, as when a storm having spent its power, sends back a fitful stream of lightning into the clear sky. It was the fearful throe of dying desperation. Hell was mad because the feet of heroes was heard on Southern soil. Because the shouts of freemen mingled with the roar of Southern forests. Because the old flag was borne triumphantly aloft, without a star dropped out of its glorious constellation. Because the great abolitionist walked the streets of the tyrant. These signs of victory, and of a nation's disenthrallment, were more than the spirits of darkness could stand. Gathering up all their spite and hellish fury, they poured it out on the nation's head. No matter who murdered Mr. Lincoln—it will ever stand charged to slavery. Because it was the spirit born of slavery. It was no more than it has done. A system that will brutalize men and women, is ripe for any crime. Slavery is the hot-bed of every damnable thing. It breeds unheard of things in the calendar of crime. And now it stands before us in all its appalling horrors. God has painted the tyrant on the heavens. Any man now that justifies slavery is guilty of the blood of Mr. Lincoln. Because it is plainly manifest who did it. The cement of fugitive slave bills will no more hold. The blood of patriot's has dissolved the glue. The great soul of this nation now demands that slavery shall forever die. But O! what a crisis have we passed! How absolutely necessary was this war. It came not a moment too soon. For in a few years more of prosperity, slavery would have placed its foot upon every threshold in the land, and set its cursed heel on every inch of our public domain. It is the very nature of crime to spread or die. Hell must have new victims, or consume with its own fires. O! think where we should have been if slavery had triumphed! We shudder even at the contemplation! Such barbarity, such crimes does it bring. We stand in view of the facts in breathless astonishment. What dangers have we escaped! In comparison, has the blood of our boys been anything—have our paltry sacrifices been anything? Better,

far better, that a whole generation should have perished, and
our hills should have been washed down with patriot blood.
than that this curse should have been allowed to conquer!
Behold the goodness of God in this war! We never knew
what slavery was until God smote its carcass with his sword,
and revealed to us its corruption. All honor to those men
who first opposed slavery. Who stood as a wall of adamant
against it. Who created public sentiment. In the years to
come, the grandest honor a child can have will be that its
father or grand-father was an abolitionist. The names of
Lovejoy, Torrey, and Lincoln will shine the brightest stars in
our national firmament. Hence it was not set of men that
made this war.

There were moral forces driving on the embattled hosts.
Men were mere puppets in the hands of great forces for good,
or evil. It is the battle of liberty where God himself led the
hosts of truth. Mr. Lincoln is dead. He bears the responsibilities of a nation's cares no more. He carries no more the
load of the nation's sorrows. He lived long enough to see the
rock of our hope strong amid the swaying billows. God took
him up into the mount and showed him the future blessedness
of the country. He looked over the sunny South, and saw
the fruits of liberty hanging on every bough. He heard the
songs of freemen, as they went forth to their peaceful toil.
He saw the tribes of every tongue gathered under the fair folds
of our flag of beauty. And over all, he saw the city of the
great King rising in the midst of the scene. When he had
caught a glimpse of this prophetic future, God took him to
himself. On the very day he died, our flag was raised over
the spot where the war began, without the loss of a star.
Grand unity of our country's destiny. Our words are una-
vailing—but the future will do Abraham Lincoln justice. En-
joy thy repose, illustrious President. We will catch up thy
mantle, and declare by Him that sitteth on the throne, that
we will protect freedom in this land, and never desert that
cause which you cemented with your blood. Over thy hal-
lowed grave freemen shall gather and shake hands in ever-

lasting friendship. Strangers shall flock to thy resting place, and drink in the inspiration of thy heroic deeds. And children's children shall visit thy tomb, and there consecrate themselves to liberty and to God. Heroes and patriots of all lands shall stand over thy repose, and unite their tears, and unite their praises. Let us all be faithful to the mighty trusts that rest upon us. We have a God, whom no danger can reach, and cherubic legions guard our beloved land. As the flag of our nation was raised over Fort Sumter on that sad Friday, so let us raise the banner of the Lord God of hosts. Let us all bend our energies to the mighty work. Let us consecrate all our powers to the salvation of our country, till this blood-bought land shall be clothed, and in her right mind, sitting at the feet of Jesus.

www.ingramcontent.com/pod-product-compliance
Lightning Source LLC
Chambersburg PA
CBHW021524090426

42739CB00007B/776